The Day Heaven Looked Backed

The Day Heaven Looked Backed

A Mother's Story

J.B. Summers

Stone Light Press

jbsummers.com
www.stonelightpress.biz

Ordering Information:
Quantity sales. Special discounts are available on quantity purchases by corporations, associations, and others. For details, contact the publisher at the website addresses above.
Orders by U.S. trade bookstores and wholesalers. Please contact distribution coordinator: www.stonelightpress.com.

Publisher's Cataloging-in-Publication data
Summers, J.B. (Joyce Summers)
ISBN 978-0-9977646-2-8
First Edition

14 13 12 11 10 / 10 9 8 7 6 5 4 3 2 1

www.stonelightpress.com

Printed in the United States of America

Contents

Acknowledgements

How do we know where our loved ones go when physical life ends? Is there a Heaven? A Hell? A light we walk towards or a darkness we enter? A "beige point" I felt myself. Will we be met by loved ones or end in nothingness? Does Divine Love really exist? Many of us who lost dear ones are filled with a surreal anguish equated to broken shards of glass scraping each nerve of our body as we search for a healing. Some go numb. Others are left with unanswered questions. Still others have been given the gift of peace, comfort and love with loss. Most find closure living in the joyful memories we are left with. For me it was all of the above and more as I tried to save my daughter's life. It became a snap shot in time permanently imprinted in my mind.

I wrote The Day Heaven Looked Back approximately 30 days after I buried my daughter Jen. I have not changed much of the original words other than general spelling corrections, periods, commas, and omitting a bad word choice or two a personal friend suggested. I knew having a professional editor would distract from the raw emotions I felt during the writing of my story of the day heaven looked back. The title was born from the truth of this story. Heaven really did look back. I was given a gift of love to share to those who need to find strength in difficult times. To champion overcoming the pain of deep grief that comes with loss.

I remember I was sharply awakened about 3:00 in the morning a month after Jen died with a strong feeling to record what happened to me. I knew I was writing more than a cathartic journal entry. My story was not an inspirational quip, but, a spiritual driven movement so others might benefit from my experience. I chronologically relived the events of the last 48 hours I spent with my youngest daughter, Jen, before her unexpected death. The Day Heaven Looked Back is raw, truthful, roller coaster ride of powerful emotions. An inspirational shocking story that gives the readers a glimpse into the great mystery of unbreakable love that transcends time, place and understanding of when a loved one crosses over.

Over the course of my three years of grief many people crossed my path with and without knowing my daughter died. My thanks to all those named and unnamed beautiful people living in my everyday world who shared this journey, Bobby Boribong, Cliff Edwards, Kate, Susan Malka, Susan Quasha, Ray Stinchcomb

A special thank you to Douglas Broadfield, PhD, Andy Holzman, MP LMFT, who gave their time to listen with extraordinary kindness, Rev. Dr. Patricia Kenney who offered graciously to proofread my original manuscript, shared in the healing of our family with poems, her presence and prayers. The Florida Atlantic University, Department of Disabilities, Anthropology Department and my angel Jen.

J.B. Summers, CPLC
October 15, 2018

Forward

Joyce Summers to me is my longtime friend since high school. I knew Jen since she was born. She and her older sister Jamie grew up with our two children, Jon and Emily. We celebrated birthdays together, saw Bozo's Circus together, went on vacation together. When Joyce and their family moved around the country, we visited them in Reno, Baltimore, and Florida.

When I read these pages that Joyce penned following Jen's death, I was startled by how much they seemed to capture the spirit of who Jen was, and also the miracle of how God is made known to us even in the most shocking and challenging of times.

Joyce does not glamorize the challenges Jen and her family faced; rather, she unfolds them in a way that lets the reader experience both the deep pain of a life lost, and the faith and hope that reach out beyond the boundaries of death. I commend this book to you, and invite you to curl up and read it slowly, journaling your own thoughts and experiences, your own questions and hopes along the way.

Patti Kenney
September 6, 2018

Rev. Dr. Patricia A. (Patti) Kenney
Spiritual Director
Ordained Christian minister serving American Baptist
Churches USA 1994-2007, United Church of Christ
2007-2018.
Senior trainer and curriculum developer, Center for Emotional Intelligence and Human Relations
Program developer, Ecumenical Center for Christian
Leadership 2004-2018.
Author of devotional articles (i.e. Women at the Well volumes 1 & 2, Judson Press)
Magazine and journal articles (i.e. the Living Pulpit, Jubilee issue)
Co-author higher education articles (i.e. Change magazine)

Introduction

In "the Day Heaven Looked Back", A Mother's Story, Joyce Summers deals with an issue that, for any parent, is their most feared reality.

Every loving parent thinks about it, worries about it and for some, unfortunately this fear becomes a reality. Losing a child, the loss of your daughter, the Death of your child can not be handled easily.

I remember my grandmother had to be restrained from throwing herself into the open grave of her son, my father, who predeceased her. It is a scene of pain and grief that is burned into my memory. The events in this memoir, not only connected me to another's feelings and struggles but also, connected me to my own past, in a way that increases realization of the power and importance of the healing emotional journey.

JB Summers relates her pain, her thoughts, her anger, her sadness, her losses and ultimately her faith and hope for both her daughter, Jen and herself in this very real and very raw story. Joyce Summers wrote this cathartic story soon after the events that transpired in August, 2015.

I've known Joyce Summers for many years, and she has despite some painful family issues, worked on being an inspiration to others. Joyce is more than her pain because she chooses the future.

JB Summers is a published author, an artist, and a scientist who has taken a painful and overwhelming time in her life and has turned it into a story that she hopes will connect and inspire others. I believe the truth and the raw reality of one woman's physical, psychological and emotional journey can help anyone who reads this to connect on a deep level to help work through personal loss and have faith for the future.

Andrew S. Holzman MPS, LMFT
September 2, 2018

1

A Mother's Story

J.B. SUMMERS

August 8, 2015. The day my youngest daughter died. This is the story of Jen's last 48 hours on this earth. Jen was a gifted pure soul who was swept into a world of inner doubt inflamed by multiple layered challenges. Jen was funny, playful, intelligent and beautiful by any standard. Who would have thought a random hit and run automobile accident would lead to incurable chronic back pain, shunned opiates, unethical doctors, and then finally, death.

Jen had championed living with severe asthma most of her life. Keeping up with the demands of university coursework, job responsibilities, chronic pain and currently her parents' divorce only added to the layers she tried to juggle. The car accident was one too many balls she had to keep in the air. Jen's anguish grew as she was overwhelmed with trying to keep up with life. She felt abandoned, rejected, and spiraling downwards through the chasms of our current health care system. She wanted to live. She wanted to die. Jen lived to love others. She loved her family, friends, her dogs, animals, our country and Jesus. Jen was a sensitive soul who wore her heart openly. Her strong faith in Jesus was what keep her alive in the last days.

She wanted to die to end the pain, but, her love of living kept her going until the pain, the rejection of pleas, the inability to express herself and partial isolation took its toll on her. Jen's mind became confused under the many medications she took to live. Her body gave out. Her "heart" did not.

Jen's medical doctors, friends, and family made harsh judgments instead of offering compassion and a healing diagnosis. Pills, cortisone shots, epidurals that at first, she shunned then became addicted to the very medication her doctors prescribed. Her death was a combination of many things; mostly of medical misunderstandings, abandonment, and a lot of pain which nicely fit together on a line prepared for the cause of death to read accidental overdose. Why? I may never know. Those who have gone through similar pain and loss may feel the same as I do as we search for reasons to give us peace in this world; trying to reason that somehow, God has forgotten us in our loss, as many had forgotten God. Good news: God and The Holy Spirit are still in charge of giving comfort if we believe and accept God's mercy and presence.

God's great gifts of mercy and light were not given only to Jen and me in a profoundly personal way, but in a "Holy" way. I was spared. I was given peace at the time of her death.

For me, this proved how a single personal incident like death reveals how the bonds of real love transcend time, space and our earthly reality to bring the peace that few experiences in the same way. As I watched my daughter cross over into the light, my daughter and I changed forever. Jen ascended, and I remained.

God is alive. Heaven is real. You are loved. One must be open to love and the unseen Light. My goal in sharing my story of loss, rebirth, and resurrection is to open those doors for you. To give you hope even in the most tragic of times.

My prayer is that as you read the story of Jen, you will find peace during grief. I offer up that last day for you, the reader, to believe, reconnect, start to love in a God who loves us, cares for us. We feel forsaken. Yet, it is us who so often forget to say "hello" to God, family, and friends in our busy world of drama. Life is short. So, take a few deep breaths, find a calm space and read the beautiful gift God gave me to share with you; the rebirth of my daughter Jen.

Thursday, August 6, 2015. 7:30 AM. After taking Jen's four miniature long-haired dachshunds, Callie, Amber, Dakota and Kayla out for their morning walk, I let them run to Jen's bedroom door to keep her company as she slept. She often slept late into the morning due to many sleepless nights struggling with back pain from a hit and run car accident four years ago. At 28 years old, her dreams of being a doctor, wife, mother, working model and makeup artist took a detour that day. Even though I was driving, we both shared similar injuries. Jen's symptoms worsened as time when on.

My injuries became chronic pain and something to tough it out for the rest of my life. Many days after the initial wreck neither of us could walk, talk much nor even function with the spinal, neurological and muscular pain. Jen's pain worsened to the point that depression began eating her away. Her cries for help mostly fell on deaf ears, her thoughts distorted by the mixture of high dose medications that treated her chronic pain, asthma, allergies, and more left her frustrated, more depressed.

I watched the mini dachshunds run up the ramp to take their special spots on her bed to comfort her and keep her company. They were her "children" and many times Jen's only lifeline out of depression to make her laugh. She so wanted to belong and rejoin in the family fun and love we once shared. Jen pushed herself to help friends, family. She took on more than she could realistically do herself. Then came the next layer. Pressures forced me into filing for a divorce from her father and my husband who asked me for this divorce one night after a hockey game to my shock a couple of years before her death. I was waiting for him to work it out and Jen to heal. Life never happens as you plan it when trouble hits. I often think I should have taken Jen and left sooner so much for commitments. It was a long-term marriage of 38+ years. The news added to her emotional pain. It was hard on Jen to live with even as a young adult. Divorce is never easy.

Living through her parents' divorce also added to Jen's need to seek help, maybe a cure. Jen once expressed a desire

to "get to the point when I can manage this pain to function
in life. Get a small house or apartment by my sister or even
Chicago. I need to be on my own." I agreed, but, how?
Plagued me.

Jen told me more than once "I cannot stand being unable
to drive myself to college, walk my dogs, and visit Jamie (her
older sister). Of course my nephews!" It was a long time since
we had visited Jamie who lived on the gulf side. A five-hour
drive would be painful.

Jen stirred a bit when her dogs cuddled next to her that
last Thursday morning. She sighed, then returned to sleep. I
closed the door. I went about my house chores. I slipped on
my shoes to get ready to drive to Chick-fil-a to pick up her
favorite chicken nugget breakfast and iced tea. It became routine several days a week. There was not much she could eat
with food allergies; we made exceptions for Jen. Her appetite
was changing. I was walking through the laundry room to
the door that led to the garage when I heard Jen say, "Wait
for me, Mom. I don't feel like being alone today." She looked
pale in her black yoga pants and a gray tee shirt. Jen began
to sleep in yoga pants about a year earlier to help support her
back and hips. All her fancy clothes from her modeling days
reduced to spandex and cotton. I can only imagine what she
felt as she slipped into a lifestyle not meant for her personal-
ity. Jen was in pain, yet, Jen's voice was strong that day.

I said, "If you do not want to change out of your yoga
pants we can go through the drive-through." They knew us
well at the fast food drive through and many times offered us

smiles and a kind word or two. It was in one way a social stop for Jen, to talk to another human outside the family. To hear a human voice that wasn't over her computer devices. Jen's chronic pain was so bad Thursday that she no longer could drive herself at this point.

We talked in the car a lot. I think back to that time I could still hear her voice. I shook my head thinking that at times it was a substitute for real therapy at times. During this time at least it was all we had. I feel bad today as I write this. I am guilty too of, well, sometimes too much talking and not enough listening for both of us. If I could take that time back, I might have been quieter.

It was a beautiful clear day. Warm– about 80 degrees that morning. Jen asked, "How was the divorce settlement?"

I answered, "Not too well. But, I have hopes we will be ok."

I asked her about her boyfriend, hockey, and her sister. Jen answered, "I haven't talked with them in a while." I was surprised. Whether it was her choice to talk or not to talk with them, I let her answer stand. Jen seemed especially down, discouraged and clearly lonely. Having only her mother to talk to at her age wasn't something I am sure she wanted to be stuck with. It was what it was. I understood how you could be lonely in the company of another, after all; my marriage was like that, lonely. This mood was out of place for Jen. She thrived off of being with happy people, Church members, sports fans, a lot of friends, people in general. Jen was my social butterfly. When she could not socialize beyond the emotionless internet, she felt her physical pain more. Nothing like human touch, sound, voice, and smile to get you out of the dumps, we both knew that. She felt forgotten that Thursday until we received a call from her sister just after we settled into lunch. Thank God for hands-free technology!

After ordering our take out, we drove to our "car picnic" spot which was a shady tree on the back lot of a large office building's parking lot. We often had small birds, animals and nature visit us as we ate. Jen expressed her feeling of being trapped. I nodded, validating her feelings, understanding her frustration at the slow pace she seemed to be healing. She was exceptionally sensitive that Thursday morning. Hopeless yet with hope. A paradox I would only come to understand with her pending death in two days. Jamie's call was a sign, I assumed, that better times were in store for Jen. Perhaps a new hope within the current hopelessness that only God can give one's heart. Jen was at peace and not at peace. As a mother, life coach and spiritual counselor to others one would think I had answers. I did not. Guilt hung over me for not being able to save Jen's life. I can't seem to reconcile these dark feelings these past weeks. I hope in time I will. For someone deep in conversation daily with God, I can only look back in hindsight to see that it was her soul's acknowledging what was going to happen in two days. Death. I felt guilty of praying to cure her. Asking for Archangel Michael to take the pain away. To have her physical body whole again. I had a dream vision a week before of Jen healing. There were so many signs and omens of what was to come.

As I write about those omens now, I know, they were preparing me for the worst to come. Still, I was unclear of what I was to endure — the death of one of my beloved daughters. I think back. My memory, my thoughts drift to that day.

Jen's soul was at peace. Her organic body was without peace as the chronic pain deepened, and ethereal feeling glowed. Jen may have knew she was never going to see her family again. One soul was sharing two kinds of pain: the one physical trying to heal and the spiritual one waiting to go home, to God's peaceful home. We ate our lunch. It was at that moment my phone rang. Finally, the call came. I looked at the caller ID. I said, "Hi, Jamie."

"Hi Mom," was the reply of my oldest daughter.

"Wow! Great you called" I said with joy. "Jen and I are underneath our favorite tree eating Chick-fil-a. How are you? What's up?" I continued.

Jen's senses sharpened as she raised her eyebrows in a happy surprise; in anticipation of what was said between her sister and me.

I turned to her as I silently raised one finger to signal I would tell her in a minute. She heard enough of the conversation to make her eager with anticipation. We would be seeing her sister and her family sooner than later.

"Hey Mom," Jamie continued. "Would you like to come up for a visit next week? Before I go back to work Friday after maternity leave. Tuesday or Wednesday would be best-you pick."

Jen nearly jumped with high hopes. Jen and her sister were

closer than most twins I knew. I grabbed the chance for the visit in the hope it would help Jen regain a dash of joy in her life.

"Sure, I'll drive up Tuesday. See ya on Wednesday and drive back Thursday. Jen's coming too."

"Okay, keep me updated…" Jamie finished up as I hung up.

Jen and I were surprised because we had not always been welcomed in Jamie's house for various reasons, that for us, made no sense, but we honored them.

I mentioned to Jen we are going regardless of cost. If God wanted us to go, he would provide, and we would find a way. It was at this time I made a statement I thought was understandable at the time, but, later would haunt my thoughts as guilt for some time. "Jen, we may need to bring the wheelchair for you if you can't walk. I can't help pick you up if you fall." Jen hated the wheelchair. She even refused a walking cane. It made her feel old and crippled. She wanted to be able to pick up her Godchild and nephews, and I assume she did not want her family to see her feeling of weakness. Many times we told her to do what her body needed and not worry about what others thought, including a few unkind medical staffers, doctors, and odd people. Sad to say, near the end, she succumbed to thoughts of these dominating, bullying, vampire-like personalities she found herself surrounded by.

Those in the pain clinics who did not offer cures, just handed out pills; those in the hospital who said "You can't be helped"; those who simply did not care and, worst of all, those who judged her heartlessly for the "social crime" of being chronically ill and in pain, which was no fault of her own — those who gave her the drugs only to then vilify her. Opiate withdraws are hard. Harder with every phase.

Compassion had left our world. So sad, because we needed it more than ever. One of Jen's doctors told her only after 30 days of occupational therapy that she was not progressing as fast as they liked and because her insurance ran out. Others told her not to come back. Money, legal issues, numbed people came between my daughter's healing and her death. The doctor(s) gave up on her. This was only one thing of many. Lies, the blame game, cover-ups, and rejections became the standard. This was approximately ten days before her death and her last hope of finding beneficial healthcare. So you can imagine how Jamie's phone call and invitation gave Jen new hope. Another chance, we thought.

My final divorce plea was scheduled to go before a judge exactly one week after her death. A random judge would determine who gets what and when. Being a "housewife," a female, I was told not to expect much. Cold. Heartless. Efficient.

Jen and I both had hoped to start a new phase in our lives. No angry husband to deal with anymore. The life I put on hold will start again. The best part would have been that I could step in without the oppressing interference of her father to seek the next level of correct care for Jen properly. Jamie opened her home to us again. We had joy for better days.

We smiled that Thursday. We made plans. God had other plans.

The remainder of that Thursday, I cooked dinner to keep the peace. It would be one of our last meals as a family. I hired maid service to clean the areas of the house we no longer could without reinjuring ourselves. The maid arrived on Friday morning early. Jen went to sleep more peaceful.

Friday morning. 8:00 AM. Friday was a good day. I did the same routine with the dogs as the day before. Jen slept in this morning until 10 AM. The maid met her on her way in as Jen left for a new pain management doctor. I wasn't aware of this. I learned later that Jen made the appointment to make sure she had enough medication for the trip to her sister's house. I was not aware of what kind of added medicine she was on until after her death. This was another turning point where, I, as well as others who have gone through a shocking loss, say those useless words of "if I had only known…" to reason away devastating feelings, ease our guilt, and seek redemption on what we could not have possibly known. I knew Jen was doing what she could to prepare for a visit with her sister that Friday morning. Little did I know that was the last day I would see my lovely beautiful Jen alive. I remember her checking out the kitchen area commenting, "What did the maid do? Still looks the same."

I laughed as I replied, "She cleaned." I watched Jen look around as if to take in memories; not unlike our old family dog named Summer. A Cocker Spaniel who passed over the "rainbow bridge" years ago. Like our dog days before she had a heart attack, Jen walked to our front walkway, looked around the house. Jen returned to the Kitchen. She looked out the windows as if to take in one final memory. It was unsettling to watch Jen behave in the same way "Summer dog" did.

I knew from other premonitions and heavenly signs something had changed in Jen. Her joy was gone. I assumed it was the medication. I knew where Jen was, standing in front of me, but, she was not who Jen use to be at this point.

The rest of that Friday, I finished packing, preparing meals for the day. I noticed after dinner that Jen was in a semi foggy haze. I assumed she was exhausted from her chronic pain. She behaved that way off and on after the car accident. I told her to lie down, and we both rested in our split beds. The beds were specially bought to ease our back pain. Jen lied down on her father's side. I slipped in to the other side. I was already moved out and was sleeping in the guest room after her father, Jerry, asked for the divorce almost a year after the car accident happened. He never was one to handle sickness or hard times well. Someone else had to do that for him most times. I understood that about him since both daughters were born with severe asthma. Jerry asking for the divorce was a shock in itself after 35 plus years of marriage. Jen did not take it well at first. He was not happy. We were injured. He could not help us. Others had his attention. Life went on.

Her last Friday evening, Jen fell into a calm state. We both did. I was relieved she was not in severe pain. We often took time to share moments. These quiet moments I felt was our bonding time. Jen shared that final night with me by show-ing me one of her means of escape from her pain as we spent time laughing in the bedroom at the live feed through her Periscope app.

She introduced me to the Periscope app as we watched someone in Paris at the Moulin Rouge Theater that night in real time. That too was surreal in its own way. We got our taste of Paris that last night. I promised Jen I would find a way to take her to all those places she wanted to go — the Highlands of Scotland, Paris, Rome, Australia, and Norway. Our "bucket list" was long. We talked and made plans to go to every ocean, every continent and exotic place on earth. It was a good escape that night to think on other thoughts. Jen fell asleep with her phone in her hand while the street music of Paris played on, muffled by her sweater sleeve. It would be the last music she would hear. I let her sleep in the master bedroom.

Jen often slept with a sweater that last week. She com-plained she was cold and feared it. It was approximately 8:00 pm when I left her peacefully sleeping in the master bedroom. I assumed once again incorrectly Jerry would let her sleep in the master bedroom and he would sleep in her bed as not to disturb her. He did not. Her father and I were not talk-ing much at that point. Nor was there much I could say to someone who had stopped listening to me a long time ago. I retired to the guest room for the night.

I felt worried free for once going to bed. Jen was sleeping, and her breathing was normal. Her father was doing his thing on the IPad playing WAR! The dogs would be taken care of so I could sleep myself. Jen and I would be seeing Jamie and my grandsons in four days. The divorce process would be over in 8 days. I had already decided to give up my dreams of being a bestselling novelist and finishing my Master's degree in psychology to spend the rest of my days taking care of my "Jen-Jen." It seemed like a fair trade to me at the time when you have a child with a disability. To pray for a cure. To dream joy will return after the trauma. It is only natural to think that way — peace and freedom for me and my daughters along with the certainty that a cure for Jen's pain would come too. The shock that the cure would happen on a spiritual plan did not occur to me.

The verse Jeremiah 29:11- I had seen on a license plate a few weeks before Jen's death came to mind that night.

Jeremiah 29:11 for I know the plans I have for you, declares the Lord, plans to prosper you and not to harm you, plans to give you hope and a future. (NIV)

I drifted to sleep feeling all was as it should be. Peaceful slumber overtook me that Friday night. I thought my plans were solid.

Saturday, August 8. 6:30 AM. The door crashed open to my bedroom. "Joyce! Jen OD-ED!" I sprung up in bed even with needle-like pain stabbing in my lower spine. How the hell could Jen overdose on her medication? What was he telling me? My mind flashed. Jen was no longer on pain medication. I was to be proved wrong. I shot up in my bed. What was going on? Jen was fine when I left her. Her father's words rang over and over. God, I knew I must help her if she needed it. To save my child's life. My God! Adrenal flooded my body. My own pain slipped into a place you could not feel.

A mother's love kicked in with the thought that the worst was happening: Jen dying. Somehow in my mind, I knew I was going to face an alternate reality. Jen wasn't dead. Not yet! No one should die alone. Love binds us even in the crossing. That is what I believe, and it is felt strongly in my family line. I repeated over in my mind — a quickening. A term we often talked about abstractly.

Frantically I screamed, "Did you call 911?" to Jerry, her father.

"No" he replied.

"Call 911. Damn it! Jerry call 911!" I ordered. Jen's father still did not respond. Her father, Jerry, my estranged spouse, led me down the long hallway to Jen's bedroom not calling 911. Rushing all the way to Jen's bedroom I kept asking him to "call 911, call 911!" I demanded he call 911 again and again before I knew it Jerry and I he stood at the doorway to Jen's room. The door was slightly cracked opened. Light filtered out. The door was not opened enough to see her. Her father stepped aside in the hallway, planted his feet and with his long arm pushed opened the door so that I could have a full view of Jen. He knew.

"Did you call 911? I don't have my phone?" I said. I stared at what I saw in that half second.

Jen was half turned over. Her hands positioned as if trying

to get off of the bed and could not make it. Frozen in time, frozen in this "I have to get help. I am dying" sculpture-like position. Pale, almost white but not yet dead maybe? I said to her father "Jen is dead. Call 911."

Jerry said, "Are you sure?" Blood raced to my heart making it pump faster. My mind grew sharper. I thought, oh my God, is he really going to make me check her body? Was Jen still alive? I rushed to her side.

"Call 911", I screamed. What is wrong with him I thought?

My mind raced back to Jen. I drifted to all the skills I learned to save a life. Flipping back and forth from logic to faith my mind raced. I questioned, was her soul waiting for her mother to be at her side? I cried out to God to save her in a heart-wrenching scream. Why didn't Jerry call 911? Why was he waiting for me? I was not aware her father had been in her room an hour before. I assumed he checked her breathing before taking the dogs out — a necessary habit that became a part of our daily routine. Of course, Jen being an asthmatic, there are days you miss checking her breathing, but, not like these days when she was in chronic pain.

My mind took control of deep emotions that washed over me. A mother's instinct who needed to save her daughter's life kicked in. The scientist within took over with its checklist. I touched her arm. It felt her arm was warm, pale. Still soft, warm I said to myself. I didn't see signs of the final stages of death. I turned her over as Callie and Amber who were hiding in the room ran out the open door. I saw little dog marks on her neck and dog licks on her face. A failed attempt as Man's or Jen's best friends attempted to help her. They could not help her. Her mouth, her face slightly swollen, I was uncertain of her breathing. Could it be an allergic reaction? I did not know. I was hoping, praying for mercy for God not to take my daughter. Jen was too young, too bright, too kind, and full of life. Like her sister, both loving. I could not live losing any one of them.

I could not know for certain if Jen was still breathing. Was she having an asthmatic episode with shallow breathing? Thoughts of what was wrong raced in my mind. Her body was dying. Her soul still present. Feeling that, I placed my hand under her nose. My mind believing it felt a breath. I screamed again to her father to call 911. He stood there while I used all my worthless life skills to wake her up. I checked for a pulse; I rubbed her legs to maintain circulation. I finally fell to my knees this time and shrieked to God to bring life back to my daughter with the determination that God would obey my request! Jen was not only my baby daughter but, my friend too as I was hers. I would have done the same for my first born. I loved them both only as a mother could. That kind of love bond between us is fused. It can never be broken.

I started CPR not knowing what else I could do. We no longer keep oxygen tanks in her room. Her father finally called 911. I was giving CPR to my daughter to the rhythm of the Bee Gee's song, Staying Alive. We were taught that was the correct beat. I did not know if she had some kind of seizure during the night. Jen was in the final stage of dying.

I did not believe it. I only knew death did not have its hold on her soul. Jen's father final called 911. He said. "Here's the phone."

I said to Jerry in those few seconds of thought, "I can't talk, my hands are busy." Her father said, "Here, talk to the 911 lady." Her father placed his cell phone to my ear, and I told the 911 officer the condition of my daughter. She told me to stop CPR; I could hurt her more. I instantly lifted my hands from her chest. My mind was running through its logic, keeping calm until finally, the police rang the front doorbell.

Jen' father left the bedroom as I sat alone with my dying-dead daughter on her bed trying to revive her with practical methods, with love and a prayer to our Savior. How Jen loved our Lord. How would Our Lady of Peace help in our hour of need now? It was at that moment heaven looked back at me at me and my daughter's dead body lying on the bed. With only my daughter's paled body and myself in the room, Jen's bedroom filled with a surreal warmth, a Oneness, a soft bright light coming from the top corner of her room began to open. I looked up while still holding my daughter's body. I gazed into the soft spotlight filling the room. Time stopped at that moment. The temperature changed. I saw my Jennifer, my Jen-Jen's soul on her way into the light. My heart sunk. All that was left was the organic remains of what was Jen in this life. She waited for me. She waited for her mother before it was her final time to cross over. Jen moved across the incline toward the light. She stopped halfway between me and the lighted door opening. Jen turned to face me and looked back at me. Her long dark hair swayed in the soft light. She was alive, free from pain and whole, as she had been before the car accident. I heard not in words, but, a knowingness , Jen said, "Mom! I'm okay. Mom! I am ok." I had never found or felt such great peace and love. It was a miracle. A great gift of love, peace, and joy came over me as my daughter took one last look back on her frail mother and the body that no longer could serve her or God's wishes on this earth. At that moment God, Jen, Love and I became one. It seemed like an eternity. Then maybe only a second.

As watched, I saw someone who resembled my mother who crossed over ten years before come out of the light and waved for Jen to come into the light. Jen smiled at me. She turned, her hair flipped over her shoulder, and she walked to what I believe we her beloved grandmother into the light. She was happy, painless and free. At that moment Jen was in her heaven, with those who loved her the most in this life. The light closed up. It was over. It is done. Jen had crossed over. This is why we never really die alone. Love or a loved one always waits for us when it's our time.

Approximately 7:10 AM that Saturday the police came into my daughter's room, not to find a crying, frantic grief-stricken mother, but, a mother who was at peace with her daughter's crossing into Love's light. The only thing left was to honor her remains in a way to bring healing and peace to the rest of our family. I stayed with her body for as long as I was allowed. The paramedics came. They took her away under a *royal* burgundy red-colored velvet cloth. The same colored velvet box a Waterford crystal angel was in that I had given her a week before. They pronounced her dead at 7:30 AM August 8, 2015. Jen wasn't really dead. Her body was to return to nature's ways. Dust to dust. Her soul lives on. She would leave me signs days afteward. She watches over me. I am at peace.

Jen, my daughter, now is with her Lord doing more than she could have as a healer in this world. Jen wants you to know her story. The deacon who presided over the visitation prayer spoke of Jen in heaven and having access to Jesus, God and the realm of angels. He asked us to "put Jen to work" by asking her to pray for us and to bring our needs to our Lord. I am not sure that would count as being a saint in this world, but, I know that the love, mercy, and peace Christ, Mother Mary gave Jen and me is offered. All we have to do is believe . So, pray for Jen and ask her to bring your concerns to God as one of his angels. If she is anything like she was on this Earth, don't be surprised if you receive a message back.

Spirit said, "Blessings, love and forgiveness to all." This *was* the day "heaven looked back."

About the Author

J.B. Summers (Joyce Summers), is a novelist, author, artist, and scientist. She is a Certified Public Life Coach. She loves the fine arts, supports educational causes that meet her standards. J.B. Summers is a lover and activist of wildlife. She studied the fossil record, stone tools and human brain evolution, dolphins, marine mammals, world cultures and spirituality.

Ms. Summer's received her Associates of Arts Degree in Maryland and Bachelor of Arts in Anthropology from Florida Atlantic University. while traveling the United States with her family, she studied at several top educational institutions such as Townson State University, Maryland. Ms. Summers took a leave of absence from her Masters of Science Degree in Psychology from Southeastern Nova University located in Davie, Florida upon the death of her daughter. She wrote *The Day Heaven Looked Back* during her leave of absence under her pen name, J.B. Summers.

Her literary background includes working with published authors, academics, psychologists, graphic art designers, along with one of New York City's top acquiring editor for her novel *Nine Days to Extinction (2010)*. She is a published Poet with the Chicago Board of Education and wrote a *Star Trek; The Next Generation* screenplay story accepted by Paramount Studios in the 1990s.

J.B. Summers lives an interesting life that spans the spectrum. J.B. Summers has been a Native American "Pipe Carrier" for decades, a contemplative mystic, healer, and thinker in her private life. She is respected for her wisdom, intelligence, storytelling and orator gifts.

Visit *Stonelightpress.biz* for more information.

Email: jbsummers.com, stonelightpress.com

www.ingramcontent.com/pod-product-compliance
Lightning Source LLC
Chambersburg PA
CBHW021122020426
42331CB00004B/586